INFORMATION EXPLORER JUNIOR

Speak Up! Giving an Oral Presentation

by Jeff McHugh

CHERRY LAKE PUBLISHING · ANN ARBOR, MICHIGAN

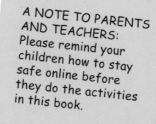

A NOTE TO PARENTS AND TEACHERS:
Please remind your children how to stay safe online before they do the activities in this book.

A NOTE TO KIDS:
Always remember your safety comes first!

CHERRY LAKE Publishing

Published in the United States of America
by Cherry Lake Publishing
Ann Arbor, Michigan
www.cherrylakepublishing.com

Content Adviser: Gail Dickinson, PhD, Professor,
Old Dominion University, Norfolk, Virginia

Photo Credits: Cover, © iStockphoto.com/PeopleImages; page 4, © Monkey
Business Images/Shutterstock.com; page 5, © Sergey Novikov/Shutterstock.
com; page 6, © arek_malang/Shutterstock.com; page 9, © Ermolaev Alexander/
Shutterstock.com; page 17, © Kamira/Shutterstock.com; page 21, © Everett
Collection Historical/Alamy.

Library of Congress Cataloging-in-Publication Data
McHugh, Jeff.
  Speak up! giving an oral presentation / by Jeff McHugh.
    pages cm. — (Information explorer junior)
  Includes bibliographical references and index.
  ISBN 978-1-63188-864-9 (lib. bdg.) — ISBN 978-1-63188-888-5 (pdf) —
ISBN 978-1-63188-876-2 (pbk.) — ISBN 978-1-63188-900-4 (e-book)
  1. Public speaking--Juvenile literature. 2. Oral communication—Juvenile
literature. I. Title.
  PN4129.15.M374 2015
  808.5'1—dc23   2014025994

Cherry Lake Publishing would like to acknowledge the work of The Partnership for
21st Century Skills. Please visit www.p21.org for more information.

Printed in the United States of America
Corporate Graphics Inc.
January 2015

Table of Contents

4 CHAPTER ONE
Getting Started

8 CHAPTER TWO
Planning Your Presentation

12 CHAPTER THREE
Research and Write

16 CHAPTER FOUR
Practice Makes Perfect

19 CHAPTER FIVE
Presentation Time!

22 Glossary
23 Find Out More
24 Index
24 About the Author

CHAPTER ONE

Getting Started

"Boys and girls, everyone has to give an **oral presentation**," Anita's teacher says.

How would you feel about speaking in front of the whole class? Some people love being in front of an audience. If you are one of these people, this book will help you improve your

Some people have no problem speaking in front of people. Others suffer stage fright!

Visit the library to learn more about a topic.

presentation skills. However, many people get nervous about giving oral presentations. If this sounds like you, don't worry! Use the tips in this book to feel more comfortable speaking in front of people. Chances are, you will give many oral presentations throughout your life, even as an adult! Businesspeople, scientists, politicians, reporters on television, teachers, and more all use oral presentations to explain ideas to other people.

There are a lot of things to learn about teeth.

To prepare for a presentation, you need to plan, **research**, write, and **rehearse**. Before you can begin these steps, you need to choose a topic. Sometimes you will be given a topic. Other times, you can choose your own. Anita's teacher asks his students to each do a presentation about being healthy. They can choose what particular topic they want to work on. As Anita takes a bite from a crisp apple, she knows her answer right away—teeth!

To get a copy of this activity, visit www.cherrylakepublishing.com/activities.

Try This

Choosing your own topic can be exciting! Start by listing six topics that interest you. They can be familiar topics or things that you want to learn more about. Next, take a close look at the topics you listed. Some might be just right for a short presentation. Others may be too broad. Narrow down any broad topics by focusing on a specific part.

FOR EXAMPLE:

Too broad: Basketball players
More specific: Michael Jordan

Too broad: Swimming
More specific: The four common swimming strokes

CHAPTER TWO

Planning Your Presentation

Once you know your topic, begin planning your presentation. The word *PLAN* can help you remember four things to think about when planning a presentation.

P urpose
L ength
A udience
N otes and Visual Aids

Purpose: Why are you presenting this topic? Some presentations give information, such as Anita's presentation on healthy teeth. Other presentations can be persuasive, such as trying to convince people to recycle.

Length: How long is your presentation supposed to be? Anita knows hers should be 3 to 4 minutes long. She will need to choose the most important parts of her topic. If you have a longer presentation, you can add more details.

Audience: Who will be listening to your presentation? What do they already know about the topic? Which details should be included to help them understand your presentation?

Your audience will probably be made up of your classmates and teachers.

Anita's friend Zack is presenting in his class about the animals that live in each layer of the rain forest. Because the class already studied rain forest layers, he can focus on the animals without spending much time explaining the layers. What if his class had not studied rain forest layers yet? Then he would need to include some information about the layers so his classmates could understand where the animals live.

Notes and Visual Aids: What items are you allowed to use in your presentation? You will probably be able to use notes, but check to make sure. Also, find out if you can use **visual aids** such as pictures, maps, or posters. Anita's teacher asked his students to use some technology, such as slide shows and videos.

To get a copy of this activity, visit www.cherrylakepublishing.com/activities.

Try This

There are many types of visual aids. You want to choose visual aids that help the audience understand your topic. On a separate piece of paper, match each purpose listed on the left with the visual aid on the right. Turn this page upside down to compare your answers to ours.

TOPIC: Australia

Purpose:
1. Learn where Australian cities are located
2. See what money is used in Australia
3. Learn how Australians throw boomerangs
4. See the pouches of Australian animals

Visual Aid:
a. Pass around Australian coins
b. Show photos of kangaroos and koalas
c. Display a map
d. Play a video

Answers: 1-c; 2-a; 3-d; 4-b

STOP! Don't write in the book!

11

CHAPTER THREE

Research and Write

For any presentation, you want your information to be correct. To do this, you should research your topic. This is a good idea even if you already know a lot about your topic. Web sites, books, and experts on your topic can be good sources of information. Librarians are research specialists, so your school and public library are great places to go if you need help. When Anita looks for information, her dad helps her do some research online. They also visit the library.

Special Web sites can help you find useful information from safe sites online. Two examples are www.kidsclick.com or www.kidrex.org.

Once you have enough information, it is time to write a draft. Organize your presentation into three parts: **introduction**, **body**, and **conclusion**. The introduction, or beginning, introduces your topic. Use an interesting fact or a joke in your introduction to grab the audience's attention. The body, or middle, contains information about your topic. Keep the length of your presentation in mind when adding details. The longer your presentation, the more facts you will need. Anita has to limit how many facts she includes because her presentation must be short. The conclusion, or ending, summarizes your presentation. It will help the audience remember the presentation's main points.

When your draft is finished, you don't want to read it word for word. If you read directly from your paper, it is hard to speak loudly and make eye contact with the audience. Instead, you should make notes. For her notes, Anita writes key words and phrases on note cards. She can look down at the note cards to help her remember what to say. Then, she can look up and speak to the audience.

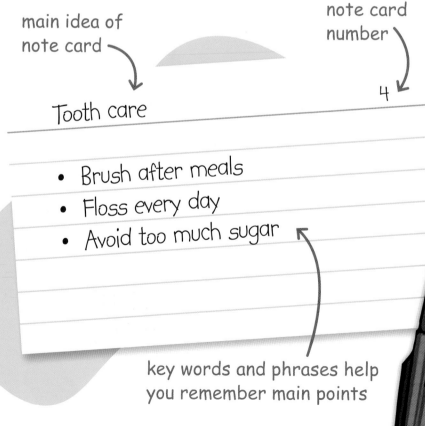

main idea of
note card

note card
number

4

Tooth care

• Brush after meals
• Floss every day
• Avoid too much sugar

key words and phrases help
you remember main points

To get a copy of this activity, visit www.cherrylakepublishing.com/activities.

Try This

Read the following information about German shepherds. On a note card, write down several key words or phrases about what makes them good pets. Turn the page upside down to compare your notes to ours.

German shepherds make excellent pets. They are great watchdogs, since they are naturally protective of their families. These dogs get along well with children. German shepherds are also very easy to train.

OUR NOTES:
- great watchdogs
- get along with children
- easy to train

CHAPTER FOUR

Practice Makes Perfect

Before you take the stage, it is a good idea to rehearse, or practice. Give your presentation in front of a mirror. You can also record it on video and watch it. Time yourself to see if your presentation is too long or too short. Practice these skills that good speakers use:

- Speak in a loud, clear voice so that the audience can hear you.
- Look up from your note cards and make eye contact with the audience.
- Use expression and **gestures**. If you seem bored with your topic, the audience will feel the same way.

Practice in front of a mirror.

16

Many people say "um" and "you know" when they speak. People use these **fillers** when they are trying to think of the right words to use. However, these phrases can be distracting to the audience. The more you practice your presentation, the less you will need to stop and think.

Anita practices several times by herself first. Then she rehearses her presentation in front of her family and friends. She asks them to time her. When she finishes, she asks them for suggestions to improve her presentation.

Practice until you can give your entire presentation without stumbling over words or pausing awkwardly.

To get a copy of this activity, visit www.cherrylakepublishing.com/activities.

Try This

Ask someone to videotape you giving a presentation or telling a story. When you have finished, watch the video. Copy the chart below on a separate piece of paper. Use this to help you reflect on your performance.

In my presentation, I . . .	Not at all	Some	A lot
Spoke loudly and clearly			
Made eye contact			
Used fillers ("um," "you know")			
Spoke with expression			
Used gestures			

Discuss your answers with the person who took the video. How would he or she rate your performance? Which skills did you do well? Which ones need improvement?

STOP! Don't write in the book!

CHAPTER FIVE

Presentation Time!

The day of the presentation is here. Anita knows it is normal to be nervous before presenting to a group. Even adults feel this way! She has confidence in herself. She worked hard at researching her topic, writing her notes, and rehearsing her presentation. Now it is time to enjoy her moment in the spotlight!

When you present, take time to prepare. Check that you have everything you need. Have your note cards in order and your visual aids ready. Take a few deep breaths. Breathing in and out slowly will relax your nerves and help you speak in a calm, clear voice.

During your presentation, be confident. Keep in mind the tips you practiced: speak clearly, make eye contact with the audience, and use expression and gestures. Many people rush through their presentations. Be sure to take your time so that the audience can understand your words and visual aids. Remember, you have worked hard to prepare for this. Go up there and have fun!

When you finish presenting, ask the audience if they have any questions. If you don't know the answer to a question, be honest and say that you don't know. You may be an expert on your topic, but you're not expected to know everything. Thank the audience for listening and enjoy the applause!

Does anyone have any questions?

To get a copy of this activity, visit www.cherrylakepublishing.com/activities.

Try This

With the help of an adult, search online for videos of famous speeches. Martin Luther King Jr.'s "I Have a Dream" speech and President John F. Kennedy's "We Choose to Go to the Moon" speech are examples of powerful oral presentations. Which skills from this book do the speakers use in their speeches?

Martin Luther King Jr.'s speeches helped change history.

Glossary

body **(BAH-dee)** the middle of a presentation that includes details about the topic

conclusion **(kuhn-KLOO-zhun)** the ending of a presentation that summarizes the main points

fillers **(FIL-urz)** words or phrases people say when they pause to think during a presentation

gestures **(JES-churz)** hand or body movements that help express an idea

introduction **(in-truh-DUHK-shuhn)** the beginning of a presentation that contains the main idea and grabs the audience's attention

oral presentation **(OR-uhl prez-uhn-TAY-shuhn)** a short talk a person gives to a group about a certain topic

rehearse **(ri-HURS)** practice before presenting to an audience

research **(REE-surch)** to collect information about a topic

visual aids **(VIZH-oo-uhl AYDZ)** objects the audience can see that help them understand a presentation

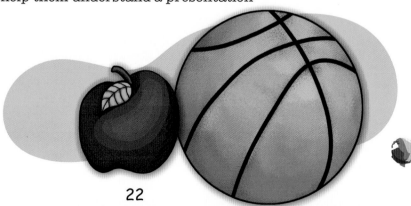

Find Out More

BOOKS

Minden, Cecilia, and Kate Roth. *How to Write a Report*. Ann
Arbor, MI: Cherry Lake Publishing, 2012.

Truesdell, Ann. *Make Your Point: Creating Powerful
Presentations*. Ann Arbor, MI: Cherry Lake Publishing, 2013.

WEB SITES

Fact Monster—Homework Center: Writing Skills
www.factmonster.com/homework/writingskills1.html
This site is packed with information about researching, writing,
and presenting.

NeoK12—Public Speaking
www.neok12.com/Public-Speaking.htm
Do you need help with oral presentation skills such as making
eye contact, using gestures, and speaking with expression? If so,
this site has lots of short videos to improve your skills.

Index

audiences, 5, 9–10, 11, 13, 14, 16, 17, 20

body, 13
breathing, 19

conclusions, 13
confidence, 19, 20

drafts, 13

expressions, 16, 20
eye contact, 14, 16, 20

facts, 13
fillers, 17

gestures, 16, 20

introduction, 13

jokes, 13

Kennedy, John F., 21
key words, 14, 15
King, Martin Luther, Jr., 21

length, 9, 13, 16, 17
librarians, 12

nervousness, 5, 19
notes, 10, 14, 15, 16, 19

planning, 6, 8–10
practice, 6, 16–17, 18, 19, 20
purpose, 8, 11

questions, 20

research, 6, 12, 19

topics, 6, 7, 8, 9, 11, 12, 13, 16

videos, 18, 21
visual aids, 10, 11, 19, 20

writing, 6, 12, 13–14, 15

About the Author

Jeff McHugh, a former second-grade teacher and school librarian, now works with teachers and librarians in Chicago. He gives many oral presentations for his job (and yes, he still gets nervous).